HOW TO READ

HOW TO READ

By
EZRA POUND

HASKELL HOUSE PUBLISHERS Ltd.
Publishers of Scarce Scholarly Books
NEW YORK. N. Y. 10012
1971

PN
83
P6
1971

First Published 1931

HASKELL HOUSE PUBLISHERS Ltd.
Publishers of Scarce Scholarly Books
280 LAFAYETTE STREET
NEW YORK, N. Y. 10012

Library of Congress Catalog Card Number: 79-169105

Standard Book Number 8383-1315-9

Printed in the United States of America

HOW TO READ

PART I

INTRODUCTION

Largely Autobiographical, Touching the Present, and More or Less Immediately Past, " State of Affairs "

LITERARY instruction in our " institutions of learning " was, at the beginning of this century, cumbrous and inefficient. I dare say it still is. Certain more or less mildly exceptional professors were affected by the " beauties " of various authors (usually deceased), but the system, as a whole, lacked sense and co-ordination. I dare say it still does. When studying physics we are not asked to investigate the biographies of all the disciples of Newton who showed interest in science, but who failed to make any discovery. Neither are their unrewarded gropings, hopes, passions, laundry bills, or erotic experiences thrust on the hurried student or considered germane to the subject.

The general contempt of " scholarship," especially

any part of it connected with subjects included in university " Arts " courses; the shrinking of people in general from any book supposed to be " good "; and, in another mode, the flamboyant advertisements telling " how to seem to know it when you don't," might long since have in/dicated to the sensitive that there is something defective in the contemporary methods of purveying letters.

As the general reader has but a vague idea of what these methods are at the " centre," *i.e.,* for the specialist who is expected to serve the general reader, I shall lapse or plunge into auto/biography.

In my university I found various men interested (or uninterested) in their subjects, but, I think, no man with a view of literature as a whole, or with any idea whatsoever of the relation of the part he himself taught to any other part.

Those professors who regarded their " subject " as a drill manual rose most rapidly to positions of executive responsibility (one case is now a provost). Those professors who had some natural aptitude for comprehending their authors and for communi/cating a general sense of comfort in the presence of literary masterwork remained obscurely in their less exalted positions.

A professor of Romanics admitted that the *Chançon de Roland* was inferior to the *Odyssey,* but then the Middle Ages were expected to present themselves with apologies, and this was, if I remember rightly, an isolated exception. English novelists were not compared with the French. " Sources " were discussed; forty versions of a Chaucerian anecdote were " compared," but not on points of respective literary merit. The whole field was full of redundance. I mean that what one had learned in one class, in the study of one literature, one was told again in some other.

One was asked to remember what some critic (deceased) had said, scarcely to consider whether his views were still valid, or ever had been very intelligent.

In defence of this dead and uncorrelated system, it may be urged that authors like Spengler, who attempt a synthesis, often do so before they have attained sufficient knowledge of detail: that they stuff expandable and compressible objects into rubber-bag categories, and that they limit their reference and interest by supposing that the pedagogic follies which they have themselves encountered, constitute an error universally distributed, and encountered by every one else. In extenuation of their miscalculations we may admit that any error or clumsiness of method that has sunk into, or been hammered into one man, over a period of years, probably continues as an error—not merely passively, but as an error still being propagated, consciously or unconsciously, by a number of educators, from laziness, from habit, or from natural cussedness.

"Comparative literature" sometimes figures in university curricula, but very few people know what they mean by the term, or approach it with a considered conscious method.

To tranquilize the low-brow reader, let me say at once that I do not wish to muddle him by making him read more books, but to allow him to read fewer with greater result. (I am willing to discuss this privately with the book trade.) I have been accused of wanting to make people read all the classics; which is not so. I have been accused of wishing to provide a " portable substitute for the British Museum," which I would do, like a shot, were it possible. It isn't.

American "taste" is less official than English taste, but more derivative. When I arrived in England (A.D. 1908), I found a greater darkness in the British " serious press" than had obtained on the banks of the Schuylkill. Already in my young and ignorant years they considered me " learned."

It was impossible, at first, to see why and whence the current opinion of British weeklies. It was incredible that literate men—men literate enough, that is, to write the orderly paragraphs that they did write constantly in their papers—believed the stupidities that appeared there with such regularity. (Later, for two years, we ran fortnightly in the *Egoist* the sort of fool-column that the French call a *sottisier,* needing nothing for it but quotations from the *Times Literary Supplement.* Two issues of the *Supplement* yielding, easily, one page of the *Egoist.*) For years I awaited enlightenment. One winter I had lodgings in Sussex. On the mantel-piece of the humble country cottage I found books of an earlier era, among them an anthology printed in 1830, and yet another dated 1795, and there, there by the sox of Jehosaphat was the British taste of this century, 1910, 1915, and even the present, A.D. 1931.

I had read Stendhal's remark that it takes eighty years for anything to reach the general public, and looking out on the waste heath, under the December drizzle, I believed him. But that is not all of the story. Embedded in that naive innocence that does, to their credit, pervade our universities, I ascribed the delay to mere time. I still thought: With the attrition of decades, ah, yes, in another seventy, in

another, perhaps, ninety years, they will admit that
. . . etc.

I mean that I thought they wanted to, but were
hindered.

Later it struck me that the best history of
painting in London was the National Gallery,
and that the best history of literature, more
particularly of poetry, would be a twelve-volume
anthology in which each poem was chosen not
merely because it was a nice poem or a poem
Aunt Hepsy liked, but because it contained an
invention, a definite contribution to the art of verbal
expression. With this in mind, I approached
a respected agent. He was courteous, he was
even openly amazed at the list of three hundred
items which I offered as an indication of outline.
No autochthonous Briton had ever, to his professed
belief, displayed such familiarity with so vast a
range, but he was too indolent to recast my intro-
ductory letter into a form suited to commerce. He,
as they say, "repaired" to an equally august and
long-established publishing house (which had
already served his and my interest). In two days
came a hasty summons: would I see him in person.
I found him awed, as if one had killed a cat in the
sacristy. Did I know what I had said in my letter ?
I did. Yes, but about Palgrave ? I did. I had

said : " It is time we had something to replace that doddard Palgrave." " But don't you know," came the awestruck tones, " that the whole fortune of X . . . & Co. is founded on Palgrave's *Golden Treasury* ? "

Since that day no book of mine has received a British imprimatur until the appearance of Eliot's castrated edition of my poems.

I perceived that there were thousands of pounds sterling invested in electro-plate, and the least change in the public taste, let alone swift, catastrophic changes, would depreciate the value of those electros (of Hemans, let us say, or of Collins, Cowper, and of Churchill, who wrote the satiric verses, and of later less blatant cases, touched with a slighter flavour of mustiness).

I sought the banks of the Seine. Against ignorance one might struggle, and even against organic stupidity, but against a so vast vested interest the lone odds were too heavy.

Two years later a still more august academic press reopened the question. *They* had ventured to challenge Palgrave; they had been " interested "— would I send back my prospectus ? I did. They found the plan " too ambitious." They said they might do " something," but that if they did it would be " more in the nature of gems."

FOR A METHOD

Nevertheless, the method I had proposed was simple, it is perhaps the only one that can give a man an orderly arrangement of his perceptions in the matter of letters. In opposition to it, there are the forces of superstition, of hang-over. People regard literature as something vastly more flabby and floating and complicated and indefinite than, let us say, mathematics. Its subject-matter, the human consciousness, is more complicated than are number and space. It is not, however, more complicated than biology, and no one ever supposed that it was. We apply a loose-leaf system to book-keeping so as to have the live items separated from the dead ones. In the study of physics we begin with simple mechanisms, wedge, lever, and fulcrum, pulley and inclined plane, all of them still as useful as when they were first invented. We proceed by a study of discoveries. We are not asked to memorize a list of the parts of a side-wheeler engine.

And we could, presumably, apply to the study of literature a little of the common sense that we currently apply to physics or to biology. In poetry there are simple procedures, and there are known discoveries, clearly marked. As I have said in

various places in my unorganized and fragmentary
volumes: in each age one or two men of genius
find something, and express it. It may be in only
a line or in two lines, or in some quality of a cadence;
and thereafter two dozen, or two hundred, or two
or more thousand followers repeat and dilute and
modify.

And if the instructor would select his specimens
from works that contain these discoveries and solely
on the basis of discovery—which may lie in the
dimension of depth, not merely of some novelty on
the surface—he would aid his student far more than
by presenting his authors at random, and talking
about them *in toto*.

Needless to say this presentation would be entirely
independent of consideration as to whether the
given passages tended to make the student a better
republican, monarchist, monist, dualist, rotarian, or
other sectarian. To avoid confusion, one should
state at once that such method has nothing to do
with those allegedly scientific methods which
approach literature as if it were something *not
literature*, or with scientists' attempts to subdivide the
elements in literature according to some non-literary
categoric division.

You do not divide physics or chemistry according
to racial or religious categories. You do not put

discoveries by Methodists and Germans into one
category, and discoveries by Episcopalians or
Americans or Italians into another.

DEFECTIVE RELATIVITIES

It is said that in America nothing is ever consciously
related to anything else. I have cited as an exception
the forty versions of the Chaucerian anecdote;
they and the great edition of Horace with the careful
list and parallel display of Greek sources for such
line or such paragraph, show how the associative
faculty can be sidetracked. Or at any rate they
indicate the first gropings of association. Let us
grant that some bits of literature have been, in
special cases, displayed in relation to some other
bits; usually some verbose gentleman writes a
trilogy of essays, on three grandiose figures,
comparing their " philosophy " or personal
habits.

Let us by all means glance at " philology " and
the " germanic system." Speaking as an historian,
" we " may say that this system was designed to
inhibit thought. After 1848 it was, in Germany,
observed that some people thought. It was necessary
to curtail this pernicious activity, the thinkists were
given a china egg labelled scholarship, and were

gradually unfitted for active life, or for any contact with life in general. Literature was permitted as a subject of study. And its study was so designed as to draw the mind of the student away from literature into inanity.

WHY BOOKS ?

1

This simple first question was never asked.

The study of literature, or more probably of morphology, verb/roots, etc., was permitted the German professor in, let us say, 1880/1905, to keep his mind off life in general, and off public life in particular.

In America it was permitted from precedent; it was known to be permitted in Germany; Germany had a " great university tradition," which it behooved America to equal and perhaps to surpass.

This study, or some weaker variety of it, was also known to be permitted at Oxford, and supposed to have a refining influence on the student.

II

The practice of literary composition in private has been permitted since " age immemorial," like knitting, crocheting, etc. It occupies the practitioner, and, so long as he keeps it to himself, *ne nuit pas aux autres,* it does not transgress the definition of liberty which we find in the declaration of the *Droits de l'Homme* : Liberty is the right to do anything which harms not others. All of which is rather negative and unsatisfactory.

III

It appears to me quite tenable that the function of literature as a generated prize-worthy force is precisely that it does incite humanity to continue living ; that it eases the mind of strain, and feeds it, I mean definitely as *nutrition of impulse.*

This idea may worry lovers of order. Just as good literature does often worry them. They regard it as dangerous, chaotic, subversive. They try every idiotic and degrading wheeze to tame it down. They try to make a bog, a marasmus, a great putridity in place of a sane and active ebullience. And they do this from sheer simian and pig-like stupidity, and from their failure to understand the function of letters.

IV

Has literature a function in the state, in the aggregation of humans, in the republic, in the *res publica,* which ought to mean the public con﹣ venience (despite the slime of bureaucracy, and the execrable taste of the populace in selecting its rulers) ? It has.

And this function is *not* the coercing or emotion﹣ ally persuading, or bullying or suppressing people into the acceptance of any one set or any six sets of opinions as opposed to any other one set or half﹣ dozen sets of opinions.

It has to do with the clarity and vigour of " any and every " thought and opinion. It has to do with maintaining the very cleanliness of the tools, the health of the very matter of thought itself. Save in the rare and limited instances of invention in the plastic arts, or in mathematics, the individual cannot think and communicate his thought, the governor and legislator cannot act effectively or frame his laws, without words, and the solidity and validity of these words is in the care of the damned and despised *literati.* When their work goes rotten— by that I do not mean when they express indecorous thoughts—but when their very medium, the very essence of their work, the application of word to

2

thing goes rotten, *i.e.,* becomes slushy and inexact, or excessive or bloated, the whole machinery of social and of individual thought and order goes to pot.   This is a lesson of history, and a lesson not yet half learned.

The great writers need no debunking.

The pap is not in them, and doesn't need to be squeezed out.   They do not lend themselves to imperial and sentimental exploitations.   A civiliza⁄tion was founded on Homer, civilization not a mere bloated empire.   The Macedonian domination rose and grew after the sophists.   It also subsided.

It is not only a question of rhetoric, of loose ex⁄pression, but also of the loose use of individual words. What the renaissance gained in direct examination of natural phenomena, it in part lost in losing the feel of and desire for exact descriptive terms.   I mean that the mediæval mind had little but words to deal with, and it was more careful in its definitions and verbiage.   It did not define a gun in terms that would just as well define an explosion, nor explosions in terms that would define triggers.

Misquoting Confucius, one might say: It does not matter whether the author desire the good of the race or act merely from personal vanity.   The thing is mechanical in action.   In proportion as his work is exact, *i.e.,* true to human consciousness and to the nature of man, as it is exact in formulation of desire, so is it durable and so is it "useful"; I mean it maintains the precision and clarity of thought, not merely for the benefit of a few dilettantes and "lovers of literature," but maintains the health of thought outside literary circles and in non-literary existence, in general individual and communal life.

Or "*dans ce genre on n'émeut que par la clarté.*" One "moves" the reader only by clarity. In depicting the motions of the "human heart" the durability of the writing depends on the exactitude. It is the thing that is true and stays true that keeps fresh for the new reader.

. . . . . .

With this general view in mind, and subsequent to the events already set forth in this narrative, I proposed (from the left bank of the Seine, and to an American publishing house), not the twelve-volume anthology, but a short guide to the subject. That was after a few years of "pause and reflection." The subject was pleasantly received and considered with amity, but the house finally decided that it would pay neither them to print nor me to write the book, because we "weren't in the text-book ring." For the thing would have been a text-book, its circulation would have depended on educators, and educators have been defined as " men with no intellectual interests."

Hence, after a lapse of four years, this essay, dedicated to Mr. Glenn Frank, and other starters of ideal universities, though not with any great hope that it will rouse them.

PART II

OR WHAT MAY BE AN
INTRODUCTION TO METHOD

IT is as important for the purpose of thought to keep language efficient as it is in surgery to keep tetanus bacilli out of one's bandages.

In introducing a person to literature one would do well to have him examine works where language is efficiently used; to devise a system for getting directly and expeditiously at such works, despite the smoke-screens erected by half-knowing and half-thinking critics. To get at them, despite the mass of dead matter that these people have heaped up and conserved round about them in the proportion: one barrel of sawdust to each half-bunch of grapes.

Great literature is simply language charged with meaning to the utmost possible degree.

When we set about examining it we find that this charging has been done by several clearly definable sorts of people, and by a periphery of less determinate sorts.

(a) *The inventors*, discoverers of a particular process or of more than one mode and process.

Sometimes these people are known, or discoverable;
for example, we know, with reasonable certitude,
that Arnaut Daniel introduced certain methods of
rhyming, and we know that certain finenesses of
perception appeared first in such a troubadour or in
G. Cavalcanti. We do not know, and are not
likely to know, anything definite about the pre-
cursors of Homer.

(b) *The masters.* This is a very small class, and
there are very few real ones. The term is properly
applied to inventors who, apart from their own
inventions, are able to assimilate and co-ordinate
a large number of preceding inventions. I mean to
say they either start with a core of their own and
accumulate adjuncts, or they digest a vast mass of
subject-matter, apply a number of known modes of
expression, and succeed in pervading the whole with
some special quality or some special character of
their own, and bring the whole to a state of homo-
geneous fulness.

(c) *The diluters,* those who follow either the
inventors or the " great writers," and who produce
something of lower intensity, some flabbier variant,
some diffuseness or tumidity in the wake of the
valid.

(d) (And this class produces the great bulk of all
writing.) The men who do more or less good work

in the more or less good style of a period. Of these the delightful anthologies, the song books, are full, and choice among them is the matter of taste, for you prefer Wyatt to Donne, Donne to Herrick, Drum⁄mond of Hawthornden to Browne, in response to some purely personal sympathy, these people add but some slight personal flavour, some minor variant of a mode, without affecting the main course of the story.

At their faintest " *Ils n'existent pas, leur ambiance leur confert une existence.*" They do not exist: their ambience confers existence upon them. When they are most prolific they produce dubious cases like Virgil and Petrarch, who probably pass, among the less exigeant, for colossi.

(*e*) *Belles Lettres*. Longus, Prévost, Benjamin Constant, who are not exactly " great masters," who can hardly be said to have originated a form, but who have nevertheless brought some mode to a very high development.

(*f*) And there is a supplementary or sixth class of writers, the starters of crazes, the Ossianic McPher⁄sons, the Gongoras whose wave of fashion flows over writing for a few centuries or a few decades, and then subsides, leaving things as they were.

It will be seen that the first two classes are the more sharply defined: that the difficulty of classifica⁄

tion for particular lesser authors increases as one descends through the list, save for the last class, which is again fairly clear.

The point is, that if a man know the facts about the first two categories, he can evaluate almost any unfamiliar book at first sight. I mean he can form a just estimate of its worth, and see how and where it belongs in this schema.

As to crazes, the number of possible diseases in literature is perhaps not very great, the same afflictions crop up in widely separated countries without any previous communication. The good physician will recognize a known malady, even if the manifestation be superficially different.

The fact that six different critics will each have a different view concerning what author belongs in which of the categories here given, does not in the least invalidate the categories. When a man knows the facts about the first two categories, the reading of work in the other categories will not greatly change his opinion about those in the first two.

LANGUAGE

Obviously this knowledge cannot be acquired without knowledge of various tongues. The same discoveries have served a number of races. If a man have not time to learn different languages he can at least, and with very little delay, be told what the discoveries were. If he wish to be a good critic he will have to look for himself.

Bad critics have prolonged the use of demoded terminology, usually a terminology originally in⁄ vented to describe what had been done before 300 B.C., and to describe it in a rather exterior fashion. Writers of second order have often tried to produce works to fit some category or term not yet occupied in their own local literature. If we chuck out the classifications which apply to the outer shape of the work, or to its occasion, and if we look at what actually happens, in, let us say, poetry, we will find that the language is charged or energized in various manners.

That is to say, there are three " kinds of poetry ":

MELOPŒIA, wherein the words are charged, over and above their plain meaning, with some musical property, which directs the bearing or trend of that meaning.

PHANOPŒIA, which is a casting of images upon the visual imagination.

LOGOPŒIA, " the dance of the intellect among words," that is to say, it employs words not only for their direct meaning, but it takes count in a special way of habits of usage, of the context we *expect* to find with the word, its usual concomitants, of its known acceptances, and of ironical play. It holds the æsthetic content which is peculiarly the domain of verbal manifestation, and cannot possibly be contained in plastic or in music. It is the latest come, and perhaps most tricky and undependable mode.

The *melopœia* can be appreciated by a foreigner with a sensitive ear, even though he be ignorant of the language in which the poem is written. It is practically impossible to transfer or translate it from one language to another, save perhaps by divine accident, and for half a line at a time.

Phanopœia can, on the other hand, be translated almost, or wholly, intact. When it is good enough, it is practically impossible for the translator to destroy it save by very crass bungling, and the neglect of perfectly well-known and formulatable rules.

Logopœia does not translate; though the attitude of mind it expresses may pass through a paraphrase. Or one might say, you can *not* translate it "locally," but that having determined the original author's state of mind, you may or may not be able to find a derivative or an equivalent.

PROSE

The language of prose is much less highly charged, that is perhaps the only availing distinction between prose and poesy. Prose permits greater factual presentation, explicitness, but a much greater amount of language is needed. During the last century or century and a half, prose has, perhaps for the first time, perhaps for the second or third time, arisen to challenge the poetic pre-eminence. That is to say, *Cœur Simple*, by Flaubert, is probably more important than Théophile Gautier's *Carmen*, etc.

The total charge in certain nineteenth-century prose works possibly surpasses the total charge found in individual poems of that period; but that merely indicates that the author has been able to get his effect cumulatively, by a greater heaping up of factual data; imagined fact, if you will, but nevertheless expressed in factual manner.

By using several hundred pages of prose, Flaubert, by force of architectonics, manages to attain an intensity comparable to that in Villon's *Heaulmière*, or his prayer for his mother. This does not invalidate my dissociation of the two terms: poetry, prose.

In *phanopœia* we find the greatest drive toward utter precision of word; this art exists almost exclusively by it.

In *melopœia* we find a contrary current, a force
tending often to lull, or to distract the reader from the
exact sense of the language. It is poetry on the
borders of music, and music is perhaps the bridge
between consciousness and the unthinking sentient
or even insentient universe.

All writing is built up of these three elements,
plus " architectonics " or " the form of the whole,"
and to know anything about the relative efficiency of
various works one must have some knowledge of
the maximum already attained by various authors,
irrespective of where and when.

It is not enough to know that the Greeks attained
to the greatest skill in *melopœia*, or even that the
Provençaux added certain diverse developments and
that some quite minor, nineteenth-century Frenchmen
achieved certain elaborations.

It is not quite enough to have the general idea
that the Chinese (more particularly Rihaku and
Omakitsu) attained the known maximum of *phanopœia*, due perhaps to the nature of their written
ideograph, or to wonder whether Rimbaud is, at
rare moments, their equal. One wants one's knowledge in more definite terms.

It is an error to think that vast reading will
automatically produce any such knowledge or
understanding. Neither Chaucer with his forty

books, nor Shakespeare with perhaps half a dozen, in folio, can be considered illiterate. A man can learn more music by working on a Bach fugue until he can take it apart and put it together, than by playing through ten dozen heterogeneous albums.

You may say that for twenty⁄seven years I have thought consciously about this particular matter, and read or read at a great many books, and that with the subject never really out of my mind, I don't yet know half there is to know about *melopœia*.

There are, on the other hand, a few books that I still keep on my desk, and a great number that I shall never open again. But the books that a man needs to know in order to "get his bearings," in order to have a sound judgment of any bit of writing that may come before him, are very few. The list is so short, indeed, that one wonders that people, professional writers in particular, are willing to leave them ignored and to continue dangling in mid⁄chaos emitting the most imbecile estimates, and often vitiating their whole lifetime's production.

Limiting ourselves to the authors who actually invented something, or who are the "first known examples" of the process in working order, we find:

OF THE GREEKS: Homer, Sappho. [The "great dramatists" decline from Homer, and depend

immensely on him for their effects; their " charge,"
at its highest potential, depends so often, and so
greatly on their being able to count on their
audience's knowledge of the *Iliad*.   Even Æschylus
is rhetorical.]

OF THE ROMANS: As we have lost Philetas, and
most of Callimachus, we may suppose that the
Romans added a certain sophistication; at any rate,
Catuilus, Ovid, Propertius, all give us something
we cannot find now in Greek authors.

A specialist may read Horace if he is interested
in learning the precise demarcation between what can
be learned about writing, and what cannot. I mean
that Horace is the perfect example of a man who
acquired all that is acquirable, without having the
root. I beg the reader to observe that I am being
exceedingly iconoclastic, that I am omitting thirty
established names for every two I include. I am
chucking out Pindar, and Virgil, without the
slightest compunction. I do not suggest a " course "
in Greek or Latin literature, I name a few isolated
writers; five or six pages of Sappho.   One can
throw out at least one-third of Ovid. That is to say,
I am omitting the authors who can teach us no new
or no more effective method of " charging " words.

OF THE MIDDLE AGES: The Anglo-Saxon
Seafarer, and some more cursory notice of some

mediæval narrative, it does not so greatly matter what narrative, possibly the *Beowulf*, the *Poema del Cid*, and the sagas of *Grettir* and *Burnt Nial*.   And then, in contrast, troubadours, perhaps thirty poems in Provençal, and for comparison with them a few songs by Von Morungen, or Wolfram von Essen‑bach, and von der Vogelweide; and then Bion's *Death of Adonis*.

From which mixture, taken in this order, the reader will get his bearings on the art of poetry made to be sung; for there are three kinds of *melo‑pœia*: (1) that made to be sung to a tune; (2) that made to be intoned or sung to a sort of chant; and (3) that made to be spoken; and the art of joining words in each of these kinds is different, and cannot be clearly understood until the reader knows that there are three different objectives.

OF THE ITALIANS: Guido Cavalcanti and Dante; perhaps a dozen and a half poems of Guido's, and a dozen poems by his contemporaries, and the *Divina Commedia*.

In Italy, around the year 1300, there were new values established, things said that had not been said in Greece, or in Rome or elsewhere.

VILLON: After Villon and for several centuries, poetry can be considered as *fioritura*, as an efflorescence, almost an effervescence, and without any new roots. Chaucer is an enrichment, one might say a more creamy version of the " matter of France," and he in some measure preceded the verbal richness of the classic revival, but beginning with the Italians after Dante, coming through the Latin writers of the Renaissance, French, Spanish, English, Tasso, Ariosto, etc., the Italians always a little in the lead, the whole is elaboration, mediæval basis, and wash after wash of Roman or Hellenic influence. I mean one need not read any particular part of it for purpose of learning one's comparative values.

If one were studying history and not poetry, one might discover the mediæval mind more directly in the opening of Mussato's *Ecerinus* than even in Dante. The culture of Chaucer is the same which went contemporaneously into Ferrara, with the tongue called " *francoveneto.*"

One must emphasize one's contrasts in the quattro-cento. One can take Villon as pivot for under-standing them. After Villon, and having begun before his time, we find this *fioritura*, and for centuries we find little else. Even in Marlowe and Shake-speare there is this embroidery of language, this talk about the matter, rather than presentation. I doubt if any one ever acquired discrimination in studying

" The Elizabethans." You have grace, richness of language, abundance, but you have probably nothing that isn't replaceable by something else, no ornament that wouldn't have done just as well in some other connection, or for which some other figure of rhetoric couldn't have served, or which couldn't have been distilled from literary antecedents.

The " language" had not been heard on the London stage, but it had been heard in the Italian law courts, etc.; there were local attempts, all over Europe, to teach the public (in Spain, Italy, England) Latin diction. "Poetry" was considered to be (as it still is considered by a great number of drivelling imbeciles) synonymous with " lofty and flowery language."

One Elizabethan specialist has suggested that Shakespeare, disgusted with his efforts, or at least despairing of success, as a poet, took to the stage. The drama is a mixed art; it does not rely on the charge that can be put into the word, but calls on gesture and mimicry and "impersonation" for assistance. The actor must do a good half of the work. One does no favour to drama by muddling the two sets of problems.

Apologists for the drama are continually telling us in one way or another that drama either cannot use at all, or can make but a very limited use of words

3

charged to their highest potential. This is perfectly true. Let us try to keep our minds on the problem we started with, *i.e.,* the art of writing, the art of " charging " language with meaning.

After 1450 we have the age of *fioritura*; after Marlowe and Shakespeare came what was called a " classic " movement, a movement that restrained without inventing. Anything that happens to mind in England has usually happened somewhere else first. Some one invents something, then some one develops, or some dozens develop a frothy or at any rate creamy enthusiasm or overabundance, then some one tries to tidy things up. For example, the estimable Pleiad emasculating the French tongue, and the French classicists, and the English classicists, etc., all of which things should be relegated to the subsidiary zone: period interest, historical interest, bric-à-brac for museums.

At this point some one says: " O, but the ballads." All right, I will allow the voracious peruser a half-hour for ballads (English and Spanish, or Scotch, Border, and Spanish). There is nothing easier than to be distracted from one's point, or from the main drive of one's subject by a desire for utterly flawless equity and omniscience.

Let us say, but strictly in parenthesis, that there was a very limited sort of *logopœia* in seventeenth and eighteenth-century satire. And that Rochester and Dorset may have introduced a new note, or more probably reintroduced an old one, that reappears later in Heine.

Let us also cut loose from minor details and minor exceptions : the main fact is that we " have come " or that " humanity came " to a point where verse-writing can or could no longer be clearly understood without the study of prose-writing.

Say, for the sake of argument, that after the slump of the Middle Ages prose " came to " again in Machiavelli ; admit that various sorts of prose had existed, in fact nearly all sorts had existed. Herodotus wrote history that is literature, Thucydides was a journalist. (It is a modern folly to suppose that vulgarity and cheapness have the merit of novelty ; they have always existed, and are of no interest in themselves.)

There had been bombast, oratory, legal speech, ba¹anced sentences, Ciceronian impressiveness ; Petronius had written a satiric novel, Longus had written a delicate nouvelle. The prose of the Renaissance leaves us Rabelais, Brantôme, Montaigne. A determined specialist can dig interesting passages, or sumptuous passages, or even subtle passages out of Pico, the Mediæval mystics, scholastics, platonists, none of which will be the

least use to a man trying to learn the art of
" charging language."

I mean to say that from the beginning of literature
up to 1750 A.D., poetry was the superior art, and
was so considered to be, and if we read books written
before that date we find the number of interesting
books in verse at least equal to the number of prose
books still readable; and the poetry contains the
quintessence. When we want to know what people
were like before 1750, when we want to know that
they had blood and bones like ourselves, we go to the
poetry of the period.

But, as I have said, this "*fioritura* business" set in.
And one morning Monsieur Stendhal, not thinking
of Homer, or Villon, or Catullus, but having a very
keen sense of actuality, noticed that "poetry," *la
poésie*, as the term was then understood, the stuff
written by his French contemporaries, or sonorously
rolled at him from the French stage, was a damn
nuisance. And he remarked that poetry, with its
bagwigs and its bobwigs, and its padded calves and
its periwigs, its "fustian à la Louis XIV," was greatly
inferior to prose for conveying a clear idea of the
diverse states of our consciousness ("*les mouvements
de cœur*").

And at that moment the serious art of writing
"went over to prose," and for some time the import-

ant developments of language as means of expression were the developments of prose. And a man cannot clearly understand or justly judge the value of verse, modern verse, any verse, unless he have grasped this.

PART III

CONCLUSIONS, EXCEPTIONS, CURRICULA

BEFORE Stendhal there is probably nothing in prose that does not also exist in verse or that can't be done by verse just as well as by prose. Even the method of annihilating imbecility employed by Voltaire, Bayle, and Lorenzo Valla can be managed quite as well in rhymed couplets.

Beginning with the Renaissance, or perhaps with Boccaccio, we have prose that is quite necessary to the clear comprehension of things in general; with Rabelais, Brantôme, Montaigne, Fielding, Sterne, we begin to find prose recording states of consciousness that their verse-writing contemporaries scamp. And this fuller consciousness, in more delicate modes, appears in l'Abbé Prévost, Benjamin Constant, Jane Austen. So that Stendhal had already "something back of him" when he made his remarks about the inferiority of "*La Poésie.*"

During the nineteenth century the superiority, if temporary, is at any rate obvious, and to such degree that I believe no man can now write really good verse unless he knows Stendhal and Flaubert. Or, let us say, *Le Rouge et le Noir,* the first half of *La Chartreuse, Madame Bovary, L'Education, Les Trois Contes, Bouvard et Pécuchet.* To put it perhaps more strongly, he will learn more about the art of charging words from Flaubert than he will from the floribund sixteenth-century dramatists.

The main expression of nineteenth-century con-sciousness is in prose. The art continues in Mau-passant, who slicked up the Flaubertian mode. The art of popular success lies simply in never putting more on any one page than the most ordinary reader can lick off it in his normally rapid, half-attentive skim-over. The Goncourts struggled with praise-worthy sobriety, noble, but sometimes dull. Henry James was the first person to add anything to the art of the nineteenth-century novel not already known to the French.

Thought was churned up by Darwin, by science, by industrial machines, Nietzsche made a temporary commotion, but these things are extraneous to our subject, which is the *art of getting meaning into words.* There is an "influence of Ibsen," all for the good, but now exploited by cheap-jacks. Fabre and Fraser are both essential to contemporary clear thinking. I am not talking about the books that have poured something into the general consciousness, but of books that show *how* the pouring is done or display the implements, newly discovered, by which one can pour.

The nineteenth-century novel is such an imple-ment. The Ibsen play is, or perhaps we must say was, such an implement.

It is for us to think whether these implements are more effective than poetry: (*a*) as known before 1800; (*b*) as known during the nineteenth century and up to the present.

FRANCE

The decline of England began on the day when Landor packed his trunks and departed to Tuscany. Up till then England had been able to contain her best authors; after that we see Shelley, Keats, Byron, Beddoes on the Continent, and still later observe the edifying spectacle of Browning in Italy and Tennyson in Buckingham Palace.

In France, as the novel developed, spurred on, shall we say, by the activity in the prose-media, the versifiers were not idle.

Departing from *Albertus,* Gautier developed the medium we find in the *Emaux et Camées.* England in the 'nineties had got no further than the method of the *Albertus.* If Corbière invented no process he at any rate restored French verse to the vigour of Villon and to an intensity that no Frenchman had touched during the intervening four centuries.

Unless I am right in discovering *logopœia* in Propertius (which means unless the academic teaching of Latin displays crass insensitivity, as it probably does), we must almost say that Laforgue invented *logopœia*—observing that there had been a very limited range of *logopœia* in all satire, and that Heine occasionally employs something like it, together with a dash of bitters, such as can (though he may not have known it) be found in a few verses of Dorset and Rochester. At any rate Laforgue found or refound *logopœia*. And Rimbaud brought back to *phanopœia* its clarity and directness.

All four of these poets, Gautier, Corbière, Laforgue, Rimbaud, redeem poetry from Stendhal's condemnation. There is in Corbière something one finds nowhere before him, unless in Villon.

Laforgue is not like any preceding poet. He is not ubiquitously like Propertius.

In Rimbaud the image stands clean, unencumbered by non-functioning words; to get anything like this directness of presentation one must go back to Catullus, perhaps to the poem which contains *dentes habet*.

If a man is too lazy to read the brief works of these

poets, he cannot hope to understand writing, verse writing, prose writing, any writing.

ENGLAND

Against this serious action England can offer only Robert Browning. He has no French or European parallel. He has, indubitably, grave limitations, but the *Ring and the Book* is serious experimentation. He is a better poet than Landor, who was perhaps the only complete and serious man of letters ever born in these islands.

We are so encumbered by having British literature in our foreground that even in this brief survey one must speak of it in disproportion. It was kept alive during the last century by a series of exotic injections. Swinburne read Greek and took English metric in hand; Rossetti brought in the Italian primitives; FitzGerald made the only good poem of the time that has gone to the people; it is called, and is to a great extent, a trans⁄ or mistrans⁄lation.

There was a faint waft of early French influence. Morris translated sagas, the Irish took over the business for a few years; Henry James led, or rather preceded, the novelists, and then the Britons resigned *en bloc*; the language is now in the keeping of the Irish (Yeats and Joyce); apart from Yeats, since the

death of Hardy, poetry is being written by Americans.
All the developments in English verse since 1910 are
due almost wholly to Americans. In fact, there is
no longer any reason to call it English verse, and
there is no present reason to think of England
at all.

We speak a language that was English. When
Richard Cœur de Lion first heard Turkish he said :
" He spik lak a fole Britain." From which ortho-
graphy one judges that Richard himself probably
spoke like a French-Canadian.

It is a magnificent language, and there is no need
of, or advantage in, minimizing the debt we owe to
Englishmen who died before 1620. Neither is there
any point in studying the " History of English
Literature" as taught. Curiously enough, the
histories of Spanish and Italian literature always
take count of translators. Histories of English
literature always slide over translation—I suppose it
is inferiority complex—yet some of the best books
in English are translations. This is important for
two reasons. First, the reader who has been appalled
by the preceding parts and said, " Oh, but I can't
learn all these languages," may in some measure be
comforted. He can learn the art of writing precisely
where so many great local lights learned it; if not
from the definite poems I have listed, at least from the

men who learned it from those poems in the first place.

We may count the *Seafarer*, the *Beowulf*, and the remaining Anglo-Saxon fragments as indigenous art; at least, they dealt with a native subject, and by an art not newly borrowed. Whether alliterative metre owes anything to Latin hexameter is a question open to debate; we have no present means of tracing the debt. Landor suggests the problem in his dialogue of Ovid and the Prince of the Gaetæ.

After this period English literature lives on translation, it is fed by translation; every new exuberance, every new heave is stimulated by translation, every allegedly great age is an age of translations, beginning with Geoffrey Chaucer, Le Grand Translateur, translator of the *Romaunt of the Rose*, paraphraser of Virgil and Ovid, condenser of old stories he had found in Latin, French, and Italian.

After him even the ballads that tell a local tale tell it in art indebted to Europe. It is the natural spreading ripple that moves from the civilized Mediterranean centre out through the half-civilized and into the barbarous peoples.

The Britons never have shed barbarism; they are proud to tell you that Tacitus said the last word about Germans. When Mary Queen of Scots went to Edinburgh she bewailed going out among savages, and she herself went from a sixteenth-century court that held but a barbarous, or rather a drivelling and idiotic and superficial travesty of the Italian culture as it had been before the débâcle of 1527. The men who tried to civilize these shaggy and uncouth marginalians by bringing them news of civilization have left a certain number of translations that are better reading to-day than are the works of the ignorant islanders who were too proud to translate. After Chaucer we have Gavin Douglas's *Eneados*, better than the original, as Douglas had heard the sea. Golding's *Metamorphoses*, from which Shakespeare learned so much of his trade. Marlowe's translation of Ovid's *Amores*. We have no satisfactory translation of any Greek author. Chapman and Pope have left Iliads that are of interest to specialists ; so far as I know, the only translation of Homer that one can read with continued pleasure is in early French by Hugues Salel ; he, at least, was intent on telling the story, and not wholly muddled with accessories. I have discussed the merits of these translators elsewhere. I am now trying to tell the reader what he can learn of comparative literature through translations that are in themselves better reading than the " original verse " of their periods.

He can study the whole local development, or, we had better say, the sequence of local fashion in British verse by studying the translations of Horace that have poured in uninterrupted sequence from the British press since 1650. That is work for a specialist, an historian, not for a man who wants simply to establish his axes of reference by knowing *the best of each kind* of written thing; as he would establish his axes of reference for painting by knowing a few pictures by Cimabue, Giotto, Piero della Francesca, Ambrogio de Predis, etc.; Velasquez, Goya, etc.

It is one thing to be able to spot the best painting and quite another and far less vital thing to know just where some secondary or tertiary painter learned certain defects.

Apart from these early translations, a man may enlarge his view of international poetry by looking at Swinburne's Greek adaptations. The Greeks stimulated Swinburne; if he had defects, let us remember that, apart from Homer, the Greeks often were rather Swinburnian. Catullus wasn't, or was but seldom. From which one may learn the nature of the Latin, non-Greek contribution to the art of expression.

Swinburne's Villon is not Villon very exactly, but it is perhaps the best Swinburne we have. Rossetti's translations were perhaps better than Rossetti, and his *Vita Nuova* and early Italian poets guide one to originals, which he has now and again improved. Our contact with Oriental poetry begins with FitzGerald's *Rubáiyát*. Fenollosa's essay on the Chinese written character opens a door that the earlier students had, if not " howled without," at least been unable to open.

In mentioning these translations, I don't in the least admit or imply that any man in our time can think with only one language. He may be able to invent a new carburettor, or even work effectively in a biological laboratory, but he probably won't even try to do the latter without study of at least one foreign tongue. Modern science has always been multilingual. A good scientist simply would not be bothered to limit himself to one language and be held up for news of discoveries. The writer or reader who is content with such ignorance simply admits that his particular mind is of less importance than his kidneys or his automobile. The French who know no English are as fragmentary as the Americans who know no French. One simply leaves half of one's thought untouched in their company.

Different languages—I mean the actual vocabularies, the idioms—have worked out certain mechanisms of communication and registration. No one language is complete. A master may be continually expanding his own tongue, rendering it fit to bear

some charge hitherto borne only by some other alien
tongue, but the process does not stop with any one
man.   While Proust is learning H. James, pre-
paratory to breaking through certain French paste-
board partitions, the whole American speech is
churning and chugging, and every other tongue
doing likewise.

To be "possible" in mentally active company
the American has to learn French, the Frenchman
has to learn English or American.   The Italian has
for some time learned French.   The man who does
not know the Italian of the duocento and trecento
has in him a painful lacuna, not necessarily painful
to himself, but there are simply certain things he
don't know, and can't; it is as if he were blind to
some part of the spectrum.   Because of the determined
attempt of the patriotic Latinists of Italy in the
renaissance to "conquer" Greek by putting every
Greek author effectively into Latin it is now possible
to get at a good deal of Greek through Latin cribs.
The disuse of Latin cribs in Greek study, beginning,
I suppose, about 1820, has caused no end of damage
to the general distribution of "classic culture."

Another point miscomprehended by people who
are clumsy at languages is that one does not need to
learn a whole language in order to understand some
one or some dozen poems.   It is often enough to

understand thoroughly the poem, and every one of the few dozen or few hundred words that compose it.

This is what we start to do as small children when we memorize some lyric of Goethe or Heine. Incidentally, this process leaves us for life with a measuring rod (*a*) for a certain type of lyric, (*b*) for the German language, so that, however bored we may be by the *Grundriss von Groeber*, we never wholly forget *Die Sprache*.

VACCINE

Do I suggest a remedy ? I do. I suggest several remedies. I suggest that we throw out all critics who use vague general terms. Not merely those who use vague terms because they are too ignorant to have a meaning; nor merely the blah of the Murrys and ʼays, Middleton and Gilbert, and the forty habitual writers around and about, but the critics who use vague terms to *conceal* their meaning, and all critics who use terms so vaguely that the reader can think he agrees with them or assents to their statements when he doesn't (for example, so good a poet as T. S. Eliot in his performance on Jonson), by which I mean that their articles can appear in staid and respected reviews without raising a riot or causing protests from subscribers. The first credential we should demand of a critic is *his* ideograph of the good; of what he considers valid writing, and indeed of all his general terms. Then we know where he is. He cannot simply stay in London writing of French pictures that his readers have not seen. He must begin by stating that such and such *particular* works seem to him " good," " best," " indifferent," " valid," " non-valid." I suggest a definite curriculum in place of the present *émiette-ments,* of breaking the subject up into crumbs quickly dryable. A curriculum for instructors, for obstre-perous students who wish to annoy dull instructors, for men who haven't had time for systematized college courses. Call it the minimum basis for a sound and liberal education in letters (with French and English " aids " in parenthesis).

CONFUCIUS—In full (there being no complete and intelligent English version, one would have either to learn Chinese or make use of the French version by Pauthier).

HOMER—In full (Latin cribs, Hugues Salel in French, no satisfactory English, though Chapman can be used as reference).

OVID—And the Latin " personal " poets, Catullus and Propertius. (Golding's *Metamorphoses,* Mar-lowe's *Amores.* There is no useful English version of Catullus.)

A PROVENÇAL SONG BOOK—With cross reference to Minnesingers, and to Bion, perhaps thirty
poems in all.

DANTE—" And his circle "; that is to say Dante,
and thirty poems by his contemporaries, mostly by
Guido Cavalcanti.

VILLON—

PARENTHETICALLY — Some other mediæval
matter might be added, and some general
outline of history of thought through the Renaissance.

VOLTAIRE—That is to say, some incursion into
his critical writings, not into his attempts at fiction
and drama, and some dip into his contemporaries
(prose).

STENDHAL—(At least a book and half).

FLAUBERT (omitting *Salammbo* and the *Ten-
tation*)—And the Goncourts.

GAUTIER, CORIBERE, RIMBAUD.

This would not overburden the three- or four-year
student. After this inoculation he could be " with
safety exposed " to modernity or anything else in
literature. I mean he wouldn't lose his head or
ascribe ridiculous values to works of second intensity.
He would have axes of reference and, would I think,
find them dependable.

For the purposes of general education we could omit all study of monistic totemism and voodoo for at least fifty years and study of Shakespeare for thirty on the ground that acquaintance with these subjects is already very widely diffused, and that one absorbs quite enough knowledge of them from boring circumjacent conversation.

This list does not, obviously, contain the names of every author who has ever written a good poem or a good octave or sestet. It is the result of twenty‑ seven years' thought on the subject and a resumé of conclusions. That may be a reason for giving it some consideration. It is not a reason for accepting it as a finality. Swallowed whole it is useless. For practical class work the instructor should try, and incite his students to try, to pry out some element that I have included and to substitute for it something more valid. The intelligent lay reader will in‑ stinctively try to do this for himself.

I merely insist that *without* this minimum the critic has almost no chance of sound judgment. Judgment will gain one more chance of soundness if he can be persuaded to consider Fenollosa's essay or some other, and to me unknown but equally effective, elucidation of the Chinese written character.

Before I die I hope to see at least a few of the best Chinese works printed bilingually, in the form that

Mori and Ariga prepared certain texts for Fenollosa, a " crib," the picture of each letter accompanied by a full explanation.

For practical contact with all past poetry that was actually *sung* in its own day I suggest that each dozen universities combine in employing a couple of singers who understand the meaning of words. Men like Yves Tinayre and Robert Maitland are available. A half-dozen hours spent in listening to the lyrics actually performed would give the student more knowledge of that sort of *melopœia* than a year's work in philology. The Kennedy-Frasers have dug up music that fits the *Beowulf*. It was being used for heroic song in the Hebrides. There is other available music, plenty of it, from at least the time of Faidit (A.D. 1190).

I cannot repeat too often or too forcibly my caution against so-called critics who talk " all around the matter," and who do not define their terms, and who won't say frankly that certain authors are demnition bores. Make a man tell you *first* and specially what writers he thinks are good writers, after that you can listen to his explanation.

Naturally, certain professors who have invested all their intellectual capital, *i.e.*, spent a lot of time on some perfectly dead period, don't like to admit they've been sold, and they haven't often the courage

to cut a loss. There is no use in following them
into the shadows.

In the above list I take full responsibility for my
omissions. I have omitted "the Rhooshuns" all
right. Let a man judge them after he has encountered
Charles Bovary; he will read them with better
balance. I have omitted practically all the fustian
included in curricula of French literature in American
universities (Bossuet, Corneille, etc.) and in so doing
I have not committed an oversight. I have touched
German in what most of you will consider an
insufficient degree. All right. I have done it.
I rest my case.

If one finds it convenient to think in chronological
cycles, and wants to "relate literature to history," I
suggest the three convenient "breaks" or collapses.
The fall of Alexander's Macedonian empire; the
fall of the Roman empire; the collapse of Italy after
1500, the fall of Lodovico Moro, and the sack of
Rome. That is to say, human lucidity appears to
have approached several times a sort of maximum,
and then suffered a set-back.

The great break in the use of language occurs,
however, with the change from inflected to unin-
flected speech. It can't be too clearly understood
that certain procedures are good for a language in
which every word has a little final tag telling what

part of speech it is, and what case it is in, and whether it is a subject, or an object or an accessory ; and that these procedures are not good in English or French. Milton got into a mess trying to write English as if it were Latin.   Lack of this dissociation is largely responsible for late renaissance floridity.   One cannot at this point study all the maladies and all their variations.   The study of misguided latinization needs a treatise to itself.